DO DIAPERS GIVE YOU LEPROSY?

What Every Parent Should Know About Bringing up Babies

Written by **IRA ALTERMAN**
Designed and Illustrated by **MARTIN RISKIN**

AN **Ivory Tower** BOOK

Ivory Tower Publishing Co., Inc.
125 Walnut St.
Watertown, MA 02172
TEL: (617) 923-1111   TELEX: 262992 ITAP
Manufactured in the United States of America
International Standard Book Number: 0-88032-007-9

TABLE
OF CONTENTS

It is the function of grandparents to be like the sun and bring
light and joy and happiness into the lives of their
grandchildren.
Just remember that if you leave something in the sun too
long, it gets spoiled rotten.

FIVE
KEY TIPS
FOR DECORATING
THE NURSERY

When they learn they are going to have a baby, many new parents-to-be run right out and spend a lot of money to fix up the nursery.
This is where many new parents-to-be make their first mistake. They do not stop to consider the five key tips for decorating a nursery.

The Five Key Tips For Decorating A Nursery

You'll want to remember these five key tips for decorating a nursery when it comes time for you to run right out and spend a lot of money.

1. Babies break things. Things are expensive. Buy things that will not break so easily. But things that are made of granite.

2. Babies should be in a stimulating environment. Happy surroundings make happy babies. And vice versa. No matter what the man in the store says, do not waste your money on black wallpaper.

3. Using stuffed animals to decorate a nursery is a good idea. Never buy more than two stuffed animals. It is a well known fact that they reproduce in the middle of the night.

4. When my baby was 4 months old, a nice lady sold me a children's encyclopedia. "Your baby will love it," she said. She was right. My baby loved ripping out the pages and trying to put them in her nose. If you want to save yourself $300, don't do this stupid, stupid thing.

5. It may be all the rage right now, but is it really practical? I don't think so. I mean, what the heck are you going to do with a digital crib?

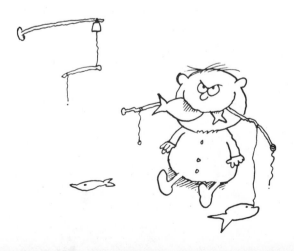

Baby's Layette:
A Guide For Beginners

Two questions that all new parents ask themselves are, "Is it too late to change my mind?" and "How can teeny clothes cost so much?"

Many new parents do not realize how many clothes a new baby needs. They think they can make do with $25 worth of undershirts, some cunning little pajamas, and a couple of disposable diapers.

Many new parents are idiots.

There are untold garments, bath aids, and bedding items that the little nipper must have.

Some Untold Garments, Bath Aids & Bedding Items

Most authorities agree that all new babies should have six each of the following untold garments, bath aids and bedding items: short sleeved side-snap undershirts, long sleeved side-snap undershirts, pull over undershirts, sleeveless undershirts, drawstring sleeping gowns, closed-end sleeping bags, non-stretch coveralls, stretch coveralls for sleeping and stretch coveralls for playing, panti-dressers, creepers, kimonos, pram suits, sacque sets (including booties and bonnets), teething bibs, feeding bibs, wash cloths, hooded towels, after bath coverups, wash mitts, bottom sheets, top sheets, rubber sheets, receiving blankets, regular blankets, tap shoes, top hats, formal pajamas, bow ties, cummerbunds, riding breeches, tattersal vests, hiking knickers, and little leisure suits.

How Much Will It Cost

Conservatively speaking, you should plan on spending between $4000 and $200,000 on untold garments, bath aids and bedding items for your newborn. You should plan on spending it again when your baby outgrows all that junk three weeks later.

How To Hold Your Baby

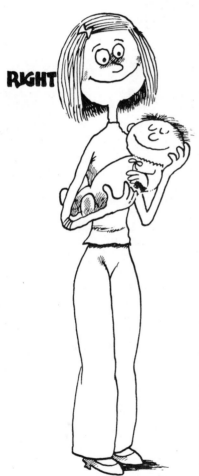

RIGHT

WRONG

Nothing scares new parents more than the prospect of holding their baby for the first time.

"It's so small," each one thinks. "What if I drop it?"

Well, if you drop it, you will almost certainly get the chair. So read this section very closely. It will tell you what the experts advise.

What The Experts Advise

The experts advise that you be careful.

"Put stick-em on your hands before you pick up your baby," says one expert. "Make believe you are holding a rhubarb pie," says another. "You'll never drop your baby if you use a fork lift," says a third. Obviously, these experts are not playing with a full deck. Everybody knows that the safest way to pick up a baby is to let the grandmother do it.

What You Should Know About Technique

Suppose one day the grandmother doesn't show up. Then what? Then you should know the proper technique for holding your baby. The baby should be face up, with one hand supporting its head, one hand supporting its bottom, and one hand supporting its legs. That leaves one hand free to clean the house, make the beds, cook the meals, and tear open new boxes of diapers, which you will need every six or seven minutes.

A big worry that new parents have is what to let their babies eat. Worry no more. Below is a definitive chart.

What You Should Let Your Baby Eat

1. Mother's milk
2. Baby formula
3. What the doctor says is okay

What You Should Never Let Your Baby Eat

1. Kentucky Fried Chicken
2. Your shoes
3. Anything containing goobers
4. Cheesecake with prunes
5. Insect pudding
6. BM surprise
7. Mao burgers
8. Estrogen cupcakes
9. Anything containing spuds
10. Olive ice cream
11. Groats, hops or kasha
12. Your best necktie
13. Suede burritos
14. Uncle Ben's instant anything
15. Albino Milk Duds
16. Chocolate-flavored Spam
17. Hot carp salad
18. X-rated Twinkies
19. Goat pie
20. Your car keys

The Truth About Midnight Feedings

You've closed your eyes
For the very first time
When the ominous bells
Of midnight chime.

Cursing softly,
You slide out of your bed
And slam your big toe,
Oh, what you said!

Down to the stove
To heat up a bottle,
The baby cries out,
Run, don't dawdle.

Back to the side
of this little pink dream,
For something so small
Boy, can it scream!

When its eaten
You gasp, "Thank God
that's through."
Wrong again, turkey,
See you at two.

The Do's And Don'ts Of Burping Your Baby

When babies eat, they swallow a lot of air. Later, that air
wants to come back out. If it does not come back out, it will
give baby a stomach ache, and the resulting screaming will
give you a headache. I know you do not want a headache. So,
after your baby has eaten, you must burp it. It's not difficult,
if you know the three easy steps.

The Three Easy Steps (The Do's)

The three easy steps to burping your baby go like this.

1. Place a towel over your shoulder, just where baby is going to throw up.
2. Place baby over your shoulder (the one with the towel), and tap baby gently on its back until it burps or throws up.
3. Throw the towel in the wash.

Many people do not follow the three easy steps, though. They do lots of wrong stuff.

Lots of
Wrong Stuff
(The Don'ts)

There are lots of wrong ways to burp a baby, and you should never do them. You should never:

1. Look directly into baby's mouth while you are burping it.
2. Burp baby over a great work of art.
3. Burp baby over your supper.
4. Kiss a baby on the lips while someone else is burping it.

How To Give Your Baby A Bath

Because it is always peeing on itself - and worse - your baby needs to be bathed regularly.

"Should I bathe my baby every time it pees on itself - or worse?" many new parents ask.

"No," many informed experts reply, "because your baby would spend more time in the water than Lloyd Bridges."

You should bathe your baby once a day.

"That's it?" many new parents say.

"Well, yes," many new experts respond. "Providing you have the proper paraphernalia.

The Proper Paraphernalia'

You don't just drop a baby into a bathtub with a washcloth and a bar of soap and say, "Don't forget to wash under your arms."

Bathing a baby is a ritual that takes time, patience, and lots of paraphernalia. You will need a special, non-skid, contoured, shallow, impact-resistant, molded baby tub, special baby soap, special baby washcloths, baby shampoo, baby towels, 26 bathmats to absorb spilled water, baby powder, a warm room, plenty of light, a big drink for later, a wet suit, a lifeguard, a life preserver, a snorkel, a shark lookout, three sets of diapers (the baby will pee in one from relief; you will drop one in the tub), three sets of pajamas, a back brace (for when you have to lift up and empty out the heavy tub of water) and knee pads.

I know that this sounds like a lot of work. But later, when they bring that clean baby to your death bed, it will all seem worth it.

The Secret To Getting Your Baby Dressed

Getting your baby dressed when it's in its first month is easy. It's like dressing a sand bag with arms and legs.
Getting your baby dressed when it's in its second month is still easy. It's like dressing a sand bag with arms and legs.
Getting your baby dressed when it's in its third month, its fourth month, and its fifth month is still easy. It's like dressing a sand bag with arms and legs.
Getting your baby dressed when it's in its sixth month is not easy. It's like dressing a washing machine agitator.
Many parents throw up their hands in frustration and ask, "What can I do?"

What You Can Do

Doctors say there are 48 techniques you can use to make getting
  your baby dressed easier. However, only seven of them really
work, and five of those are questionable. What do doctors know?

1. Hire a patient old man. (might work)
2. Hog tie your baby to the changing table. (won't work)
3. Hire the Pittsburgh Steelers to hold your baby still.
   (won't work)
4. Wait until your baby is old enough to dress itself. (won't work)
5. Wait until your baby falls asleep. (might work)
6. Throw yourself at your baby's feet and beg for mercy.
   (never works)
7. Sigh and do your best. (won't work)

How To Diaper Your Baby

How To Never Diaper Your Baby

The Six Most Often Asked Questions About Diapers

1. Do diapers give you leprosy?

Of course diapers don't give you leprosy. What hog wash.
Diapers give you hives. It's the poopy and the peepee that give
you the leprosy.

2. Why do diapers smell?

Diapers do not smell. They do not have noses. If they had noses,
they would smell. Then, they could tell when something
unpleasant was about to happen, and they would get out of the
way. Which is why they don't give diapers noses. Which is why
they don't smell.

3. Why do diapers get stuck in the toilet?

Because that's where people most frequently put them. If more
people put them in blenders and toasters, they would get stuck
there, too.

4. How can I tell when a diaper needs to be changed?

Whan the odor knocks you to the floor.

5. What will happen if I don't change a diaper in time?

You will get knocked to the floor.

6. Why are diapers white?

Because yellow and brown were already taken.

Five Unorthodox Ways To Dispose Of A Dirty Diaper

1. Put it in a large manila envelope and mail it to your Congressman.
2. Wrap it in attractive paper and let someone steal it from you on the subway.
3. Leave it under someone's windshield wiper.
4. Scotch tape it to your neighbor's dog.
5. Drop it into your garbage disposal.

Eight Sure-Fire Ways To Make Your Baby Laugh

Few things in this world bring as much joy to the hearts of parents as seeing their baby laugh.

The problem is, though, that they will never laugh when you want them to.

They will never laugh when you have come home at the end of a long day at work and need a good laugh, even if you shake their cribs and scream, "Laugh, dammit."

They will never laugh when you go into their rooms early in the morning, cooing their names and glad to see them. Mostly they will pee and ask for breakfast.

And they will especially never laugh when you are bragging to company about how nice it is to hear them laugh. The little buggers clam up like captured spies.

What should you do? Try any of the eight sure-fire techniques for making your baby laugh.

The Eight Sure-Fire Techniques

All of these techniques for making your baby laugh always work. You can be guaranteed of a laugh in return if you:

1. Ask your baby to loan you $250.
2. Try to get into your pre-pregnancy clothes.
3. Hold your spouse's head in your mouth.
4. Show your baby how you look without a girdle.
5. Smash your finger with a hammer and turn purple trying to keep from swearing.
6. Accidentally walk into a door.
7. Go along with the joke when baby takes a whiz on your lap.
8. Leave baby alone in a room and make it think no one else is around.

HOW TO
TELL WHAT BABY
IS THINKING

All Babies Who Look Like:	Are Thinking About:
	Eating
	Sleeping
	Peeing
	The Crimean War
	Having to take piano lessons
	Daddy's breath in the morning
	The point spread for the big game
	Mommy's breath anytime

HOW TO UNDERSTAND WHAT YOUR BABY IS SAYING

Those funny noises and gurgling sounds you hear coming from your baby are not just funny noises and gurgling sounds. They are baby's attempts to communicate with you. Do not brush off these funny noises and gurgling sounds as gibberish. Try to understand what baby is trying to tell you.

You can do that by conducting years and years of personal research into baby noises, or you can use the convenient chart below. It's up to you.

Convenient Chart

When your Baby Is Saying This:	It Really Means This:
Goo	Hi, y'all.
Goo goo	I think you did a swell job on the nursery.
Goo goo goo	Except for the way you coordinated the rug and the wallpaper.
Goo ga	What the heck. I bet you're really good at something.
Goo ga ga	So what's for supper?
Ga	Did you hear the one about the pig and the parrot?
Ga ga	Uh oh.
Ga ga goo	I have to do a number one.
Ga ga ga	I have to do a number two.
Yuuch	I just did a number one **and** a number two
Waaaaahhh	Feed me.
Bleechhh	You have moose breath.

THE BEST
AND
WORST
OF BABY TOYS

The best baby toys are the ones you buy assembled.
The worst baby toys are the ones you buy unassembled.
Don't ever forget that. Later, there will be a test.

Baby Toy Test

Which is the best baby toy?

Which is the worst baby toy?

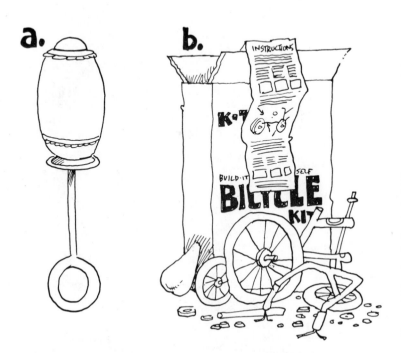

a.

b.

INSTRUCTIONS

K·7

BUILD·IT SELF
BICYCLE
KIT

WHAT TOYS BABIES REALLY LOVE

Babies really love my wife's nose.
Oh, you can go out and buy them rattles and stuffed animals and activity centers and musical mobiles and bathtub toys and the like. And they may show fleeting interest in all that stuff.
But for a toy which will catch and rivet their attention, nothing yet invented can beat my wife's nose.
Babies like to pull it and twist it; they like to put it in their mouths and teethe on it. They like to clench it in their little fists when they go to sleep and grip onto it when they are trying to stand up.
And it's really convenient, too, because my wife always remembers to take it with her and never leaves it in restaurants or loses it under the car seat. So the baby always has something to play with, not matter where she and my wife go.
Now, my wife and I have talked it over, and she has agreed that in the interest of your baby's happiness, she will sell you her nose.
But you should only buy it if you have tried to make your baby happy with lots of other toys, and have failed.
Simply send a check for $5,000 to Your Wife's Nose, c/o the publisher of this book and at the address listed in the front.
Then you'll see what happiness is.

WHAT TOYS BABIES REALLY HATE

Babies hate toys that are bigger than they are,
Babies hate toys that go "BOO!" or explode.
Babies hate toys that require decisions,
Babies hate toys they can't punch, kick or throw.

Babies hate toys that make noises like jackals,
Babies hate toys they can't suck, rip or break.
Babies hate toys that may pinch them or sock them,
Babies hate toys that go "HISSSSSSS" like a snake.

Babies hate toys that chew back when they chew them;
Babies hate toys that play songs they don't like.
Babies hate toys that blurt out when they touch them,
"Buzz off, milk breath, hit the road, take a hike."

TAKING YOUR BABY SHOPPING: A Survival Guide

About six weeks after babies are born, mothers suddenly take leave of their senses and decide to take baby shopping, just to get out of the house.

It sounds very easy to say, "I think I will take the baby and go to the supermarket."

It also sounds very easy to say, "I thing I will take a shovel and dig the Panama Canal."

In both instances, there are certain preparations you have to make.

Certain Preparations You Have To Make

Before you pack the baby into the car and head for the store, you had better make sure you have certain things with you. You had better make sure you have:

1. At least four bottles of formula, bottle covers, and spare nipples.
2. Backup pacifiers (for when baby drops the clean ones on the floor).
3. One diaper for every 15 minutes you are going to be out.
4. Three spare changes of clothes for the baby, one spare change of clothes for you.
5. Small toys, picture books, and security blankets.
6. Paper towels or tissues.
7. A really big diaper bag to put all of that in.
8. A native bearer to carry the really big diaper bag.
9. A really big drink waiting for you when you get home.

What To Do With Baby When You Get To The Store

Maybe you thought baby could skip along next to the shopping cart as you wheeled it up and down the aisles, saying cute things and getting strangers to tickle it under the chin.

Wrong, pablum breath.
You are going to have to carry baby, along with the really big diaper bag.
Some people like to carry baby on their back in a knapsack.
Some people like to carry baby slung across their chest in a hugger.
Some people like to put baby in the shopping cart and carry the groceries on their back in a knapsack.
Some people like to do all of their shopping at the drive-up window at MacDonald's.
Some people aren't as dumb as they look.
Some Helpful Hints
What you need to get you through the ordeal of shopping with baby are some helpful hints.
Let me know if you have any, because I sure don't.

HOW TO
TAKE
BABY PICTURES

Taking baby pictures is an art that few master and even fewer
live to tell about.

It requires a little skill, a lot of luck, and $800 in camera
equipment and lighting accessories.

But the investment is worth it, because through the magic of
photography you will capture forever the innocent, poignant,
happy moments of your baby's early life. You will also acquire
a storehouse of deeply personal memories and a headache
that will linger until you are 47.

All you really need to know is how to pose your baby.

How To Pose Your Baby

There are three ways to pose your baby.

1. On its stomach.

2. On its back.

3. Braced in a sitting position against a wall.

Then What?

Then you wait for your baby to do something cute.

BABY FIRSTS:
A Photo Album

(IN THIS SPACE PUT BABY'S FIRST PICTURE)

My First Toy

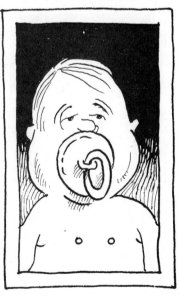

My First Poopie

**Mommy and Daddy
After My First Day Home**

My First Pacifier

My First Temper Tantrum

My First Spanking

My First Time Sitting

My First Time Crawling

My First Step

My First Tooth

My First Teething Ring

My First Broken Lamp

BABY APTITUDE TEST:

How to Tell What Your Baby Will Grow Up To Be

Show the abstract form on the facing page to your baby.

If Your Baby:
Tears it up
Tears it up, then puts it back together
Scribbles on it
Throws up on it
Hides it in its diaper
Drools on it
Gets angry and sends you to your room
Scratches its head and looks like it doesn't understand

Then Your Baby Will Be:
A bank loan officer

A plastic surgeon
A famous author
An art critic
A shoplifter
A sex maniac

A judge

The President of the United States

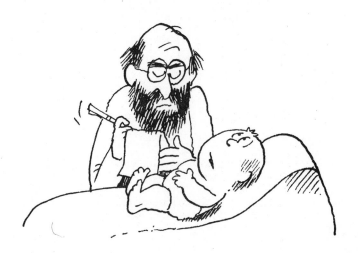

TEACHING YOUR BABY TABLE MANNERS

This is a picture of a baby who has never been taught
manners. It's not a pretty sight, is it?
Do you think this baby really enjoys playing with its food? Do
you think it enjoys dumping oatmeal on its head, smearing
carrots on the wall, and flinging applesauce across the room?
I put it to you, new parents. Is this a baby who is having a good
time? I mean, deep down. Deeper than that. Deeper.
No, new parents, this is a baby who is crying out for guidance,
for discipline, for the firm hand of love.
You owe it to this baby to teach it how to behave at the table.

How To Teach Your Baby To Behave At The Table

The best way to teach baby how to behave at the table is to eat along with baby. Show baby how silly it is acting. When baby puts a spoonful of beans in its hair, you put a spoonful of beans in your hair. When baby scoops up mashed potatoes and crams them into its nose, you scoop up mashed potatoes and cram them into your nose.

Dribble, spill, wipe, drool, and throw right along with your baby. Your baby will become so disgusted that it will immediately adopt impeccable table manners.

You, on the other hand, will take on the appearance of a gargoyle, when you rediscover how much fun playing with your food can be.

HOW TO GET YOUR BABY TO GO TO SLEEP

Putting your baby to bed and getting your baby to go to sleep are two entirely different things, as anyone who has ever had a baby will tell you.

You can put your baby to bed at 6 p.m., but your baby may not go to sleep until 2 a.m. Which means that you will not go to sleep until 2 a.m.

If you like going to sleep at 2 a.m., and not eating supper and not ever relaxing and not seeing another adult or carrying on a grown-up conversation until your baby grows up and goes to college, then do not read the rest of this section. You probably do not care about the five treasured secrets for getting a baby to go to sleep.

The Five Treasured Secrets For Getting Your Baby To Go To Sleep

Parents down through the ages have been using these five treasured secrets for getting their babies to go to sleep. Don't blame me if they don't work. I usually stay up until 2 a.m.

1. Hum softly to your baby until all your saliva dries up and your tongue falls out from the vibration.
2. Yawn deeply and say, "Well, guess it's time to hit the old sack." Say this about 500 times, or until 2 a.m.
3. Sing "Old Man River." Babies like those real low notes. You'll like singing the words, "I get weary and sick of trying."
4. Lie down on the floor next to the crib and pretend to go to sleep yourself. Most of the time, you will not be pretending.
5. Take baby for a ride in the car. The rocking motion always puts them to sleep. (And the trip from the car to the house always wakes them up; but you will at least have a few moments of blissful silence.)

HOW TO GET YOUR BABY TO TAKE A NAP.

There are two kinds of babies.
There are babies who take a nap every day,
like clockwork.
And there are babies who refuse to take a nap every day, like
clockwork.
Naps are important. They give baby a chance to recharge its
little batteries, and they give Mommy a chance to pack her
suitcase so she can run away from home.
When babies do not nap, they get cranky, and a cranky baby
is not a pleasant baby.
When babies do not nap, Mommies get cranky, and as
William Shakespeare said,
"Hell hath no fury like a cranky Mommy."
There are certain ways to get your baby to take a nap, and it is
important to know about them.

Certain Ways To Get Baby To Take A Nap

All of the certain ways to get your baby to take a nap can be divided into three categories.

1. The Bing Crosby Approach — Put your baby in a darkened room tuck it securely into its crib, and croon softly until it nods off. You may have to sing for three or four hours, but believe me, one of you will fall asleep.
2. The John Wayne Approach — Put your baby in a darkened room, tuck it securely into its crib, and say sternly, "Kid, this room ain't big enough for both of us, so I'm leaving. I'm gonna be back in five minutes, and if you know what's good for ya', you'll get yourself some shut-eye. Savvy?" That'll make the little sucker shape up.
3. The Elvis Presley Approach — Put the little critter in your lap and rock until your pelvis falls off.

BABY'S FIRST BEDTIME STORY

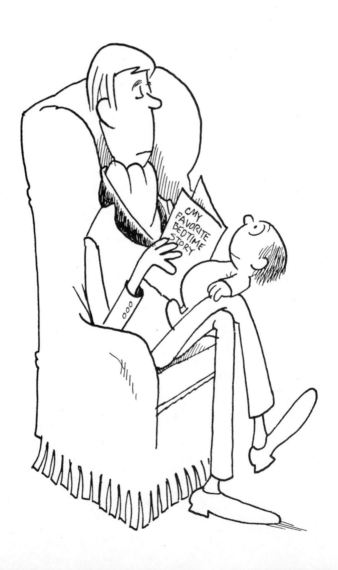

This is a lambie.

This is a duckie.

These are some dice.

Are you feeling lucky?

This is the Sandman.

He ran into a tout.

I hope, like the Sandman,

You now are crapped out.

THE PROS AND CONS OF GIVING YOUR BABY A PET

Sometimes new parents take leave of their senses (it must be the lack of sleep) and decide to buy their baby a pet. Sometimes they decide to buy their baby a small pet, like a cat or a goldfish. Sometimes they decide to buy their baby a large pet, like a dog.

Yet, they never stop to consider the pros and cons of giving their baby a pet.

The Pros and Cons of Giving Your Baby a Pet

There are numerous pros and cons to consider before giving your baby a pet. Will the pet protect your baby (a pro), or will the pet place the baby in a perpetual state of terror (a con)? Will the pet show the baby affection (a pro), or will the pet be jealous and do things like try to take the baby's food (a con, especially if the baby is being breast fed)?

Will the pet require a minimum of care (a pro), or will the pet be a royal pain in the you-know-what (a con).

Will the pet be easy to housebreak (a pro), or will the pet vie for top honors in the Most Bowel Movements Produced, In-Doors category of the annual This Disgusting Housecontest (a con)?

Will the pet willingly play second fiddle to the baby (a pro), or will the pet constantly fight for your attention, doing things like lying on the baby so that it gets some affection first (a con)?

Will the pet mind having the baby maul it regularly (a pro) or will the pet be a fink and call the ASPCA (a con)?

Will the pet take a hint and run away from home (a pro), or will the pet take over and make you run away from home (a con)?

WHAT TO DO WHEN YOUR BABY GETS SICK

All the experts tell you that if your baby gets sick, the worst
thing to do is panic.
But who are you going to listen to? The experts, or a
total stranger?
Believe me. When your baby gets sick, the best thing you've
got going for you is panic.
Panic makes you call the doctor at three in the morning.
Panic makes you fly in the specialist from Houston.
Panic keeps you awake all night, pacing the floor
and praying.
Panic is your friend.
Panic will help you cope with what usually happens when you
take your baby to the pediatrician.

What Usually Happens At The Pediatricians

What usually happens at the pediatricians is that the doctor will examine the baby, remain completely calm, and tell you everything will be okay in a few days. He will tell you to take the baby home and call him in a few days if things get worse. He will tell you that the baby does not need any medication. If you were also calm, which is what the experts want you to be, you would nod in agreement, pick up your baby, and go home.
But if you panic, you will do what all good parents should do. You will grab the pediatrician by the throat and squeeze until he gives you some medicine that will make your baby feel better in five minutes.

What Usually Happens After Your Baby is Better

What usually happens after your baby is better is that you will complain that the pediatrician's bill is too high.

GIVING YOUR BABY MEDICINE

Babies do not like to take medicine. They are small; they are not stupid.

If you have ever tried to give medicine to a baby, you know how easy getting a camel through the eye of a needle is by comparison.

Babies thrash and spit and bring new meaning to the word "stubborn." They shake their little fists and think mean little baby thoughts and get downright uncooperative whenever you approach them with a pill or teaspoon of medicine.

Grown parents have been known to cower or run for cover when a little baby vents its feelings about taking medicine.

All of which is quite unnecessary, if you know the tricks of the trade.

The Tricks of The Trade

There are five very simple ways to get a baby to take its medicine that will completely eliminate any fuss and bother. And I have statistics here which prove that almost 12 percent of these ways work nearly 8 percent of the time.

1. Stick baby's pill in a lump of margarine. (What the hell; it works with beagles.)
2. Tell baby it is going to have an ice cream soda, put a straw in its mouth, and blow the pill in when baby is not looking.
3. First take the pill yourself, to show baby how good it is. Repeat as often as necessary. (Caution: while it is unlikely that you will overdose on baby aspirin, you may develop an insatiable urge for pablum.)
4. Hold your breath until you turn blue, and while baby is chuckling with satisfaction slam dunk the pill down its throat.
5. Give baby a choice. Smoke an eight-cent cigar and tell baby it can either take the pill or kiss you on the lips.

BABY'S FIRST STEP: SAYING GOODBYE TO YOUR BREAKABLES

All parents look forward to the day baby will take its first step.

"Oh," they think. "We will remember this day forever." And they are right.

Because it will mark the beginning of a period of destruction that can only be equated to the sacking of ancient Rome by wave upon wave of crazed Vandal hordes.

Before, when baby could only crawl, it could only destroy things that were very close to the ground, like table legs, shoes, house plants, and the odd cat.

But when baby begins to walk, there is so much more to break. There are lamps and glass bowls and dishes and eyeglasses and heirlooms and chairs and crystal vases and silver trays and whatever else you have in your house that can not survive a force that is equivalent to a head-on, high-speed locomotive collision.

There are three choices you can make.

Three Choices You Can Make

If you want to keep your now-walking baby from turning your house into a replica of a jet plane crash site, there are three options you can choose from.

1. Put everything up high — real high. And remember that a walking baby is also a climbing baby. You will be surprised to what heights a baby will go to break a valuable thing. So when you put your stuff up real high, don't put it where baby can climb up and get it. Put it someplace inaccessible, like the roof of your house.

2. Lock everything away — a way away. Just putting all your breakables in a hutch or a china cabinet or a closet is not good enough. Do you have any idea how many babies break into hutches and chine cabinets and closets each year? Why, reform schools across the country are filled with them. So when you lock your stuff away, don't lock it where baby can break in and get it. Lock it someplace really secure, like the vault of the Chase Manhattan Bank.

3. Accept the will of the Fates. Many parents just throw up their hands and say, "Hey, I'm not locking all my stuff up or hiding it away. That's too much trouble. I think I will take my chances and accept the will of the Fates. Whatever happens will happen." Which is why you see so many parents out shopping for new breakable stuff all the time.

THE TRUTH ABOUT CAR TRIPS

The truth about car trips with babies is that you never finish packing for them. From the time your baby is old enough to ride in a car seat, you are constantly loading and unloading diaper bags, car refrigerators, toy boxes, dirty diaper bags, trash bags, and teething biscuit containers.

Getting ready for a car trip with baby is like getting ready for a two-month jungle safari. Except that baby needs more stuff.

WHAT BABY NEEDS FOR A CAR TRIP

What Baby Needs For A Car Trip

It doesn't matter whether you are going out for five minutes or five hours. There are still certain things that a baby needs for a car trip.

A baby needs: a car seat, a portable bed, a portable high chair, a car refrigerator for keeping baby food and baby formula in, baby food and baby formula, rattles, dolls, balls, books, baby bottles, a regular pacifier and a back-up pacifier, boxes of diapers, containers of wipes, tubes of diaper rash ointment, baby powder, spare sleepers, spare outfits, spare blankets, spare hats, teething rings, teething biscuits, plastic bags to put dirty diapers into, paper bags to put trash into, and a straight jacket to put daddy and mommy into.

HOW TO COPE WITH THIS PROBLEM

How To Cope With This Problem

There is only one way to cope with this problem. All parents with small babies should move into mobile homes.

AND THEN COMES THAT WONDERFUL DAY WHEN YOUR BABY DISCOVERS POOPIES

And believe me. It is a brown day indeed.

See, babies, as they get older, get more curious. They like to touch many things and see how they feel. The scientific term for this is "touching many things to see how they feel."

Sooner or later, after they have touched everything in their crib and within reach of their crib, they reach into their diapers and touch their poopies.

"Oooh, yucky," you say? You haven't even heard the best part yet.

There is a little Rembrandt in every newborn baby; that is to say, an urge to express its artistic being through visual representation. In other words, some artists paint crap.

Babies paint *with* crap.

It is not a pretty picture.

HOW TO KEEP BABY FROM PAINTING WITH POOPIES

How To Keep Baby From Painting With Poopies

Many parents try many different things to keep their babies
from painting with poopies.
Some make their babies wear boxing gloves, so they cannot
reach into their diapers to get at the poopies.
Some use mason jars instead of boxing gloves.
Some never let their babies out of sight and change diapers as
soon as anything happens.
Some shrug their shoulders and hope the phase passes
quickly.
Some shrug their shoulders and hire a maid.
Take your pick.

DADDY AND BABY: THEIR FIRST DAY ALONE

Every now and again, your average American mother will go
out and leave your average American father alone with your
average American baby.
Eventually, fathers get used to this sort of abuse, but the first
time it happens both father and baby can be left with deep
and permanent psychological scars.
That can be avoided, if only fathers take the necessary
precautions.

THE NECESSARY PRECAUTIONS

The Necessary Precautions

When they know in advance that their wives are going to leave them alone with the baby, there are several things fathers can do to assure that everything will be okay.
They can:
1. Leave first.
2. Beg baby to sleep the whole time Mommy is gone.
3. Call in a neighbor to help.
4. Call in a grandparent to help.
5. Not let Mommy out of the house until baby has eaten and has had a bowel movement.
6. Whimper so pitifully that Mommy will break down and take baby with her.

WHAT IF NONE OF THIS STUFF WORKS

What If None Of This Stuff Works

If none of this stuff works, fathers have one, time-tested
strategy to fall back on.
Merely refuse to stay home alone with baby, pointing out that
taking care of babies is woman's work.
For more advice, see the subsequent chapter on "Sleeping On
The Couch For The Rest Of Your Life."

OH GLORIOUS DAY: BABY'S FIRST WORD

One of the most rewarding moments in all of parenthood is
when baby says its first word.

Parents wait anxiously for this magic moment, wondering
what it is that baby will finally say, curious to know how baby
will sound.

There are many false alarms.

"He said, 'Daddy.' I know he said 'Daddy.' Come on, baby, say
'Daddy.' I know you can do it."

Or, "Honest to god, this kid said 'refrigerator.' Really. I was
standing right here. 'Refrigerator.' Or something like that.
I think."

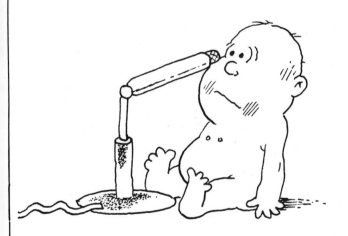

Soon, panic will set in.
"All the other babies in the neighborhood are talking, except
for ours. What if something is the matter? What if we've done
something wrong? What are we going to do?"
Until, out of the blue, it will happen. You will walk into baby's
room, and baby will look up at you and say "Hi," or "Ma," or
"Da." And that special little voice will take your breath away.
And suddenly, it will all be worth it.

WHAT TO DO WHEN YOUR BABY CRIES

Some new parents go to pieces when their baby cries. They do not know what they should do.

Some parents spend too much time fretting and saying stupid things like, "Hush, hush, baby. Everything will be all right." Or, "There there, there, there."

Babies don't want to hear this drivel. They want you to do something. So then next time your baby cries, run out and buy it a Pontiac.

AND NOW A FEW WORDS ABOUT GRANDPARENTS

It is the function of grandparents to be like the sun and bring light and joy and happiness into the lives of their grandchildren.
Just remember that if you leave something in the sun too long, it gets spoiled rotten.

BABY'S
FIRST
YEAR

BABY'S FIRST YEAR: what to expect during THE FIRST MONTH

Do not expect much to happen in the first month of your baby's life. Baby will get a lot of practice being small. Beyond that, the first month is a total wash out.

BABY'S FIRST YEAR:
what to expect during
THE SECOND MONTH

The second month is exactly like the first month, except that by this time baby will be having regular bowel movements. Nothing like the first few weeks of baby's life when there were no bowel movements, and you thought, "Gee, maybe it won't happen to us." Yes, the second month is a big bowel movement month.

BABY'S FIRST YEAR: what to expect during THE THIRD MONTH

This is a time of major adjustment for baby. As its senses of sight, sound, and taste develop it will begin to wonder, "What the hell am I doing here? They told me I was going to get rich parents." And it will try to leave. You will think to yourself, "Isn't this cute. Baby is trying to move. Isn't my baby smart." But movement in the third month is not a sign of intelligence. It is a sign of rejection.

BABY'S FIRST YEAR: what to expect during THE FOURTH MONTH

Things will definitely start to perk up now. That little blob of cottage cheese will begin to make cooing sounds, which in turn should give way to the first rudiments of formal language. You will imagine that you hear baby saying actual phrases, like, "Hi, dog breath," and "I want a Harley." Who knows; maybe you will. Baby's appetite will sharpen during this period, as will baby's teeth. Now is a good time for Mom to get those breast guards you've been talking about.

BABY'S
FIRST YEAR:
what to expect during
THE FIFTH MONTH

Baby's motor skills should be advanced enough by
now so that simple activities like using a walker,
dealing from the bottom of the deck, and imitating
Jerry Lewis can be mastered. Despite these
advances, baby's forte will remain peeing at random.

BABY'S FIRST YEAR:
what to expect during
THE SIXTH MONTH

Muscle coordination should be sufficiently enhanced for baby to begin demonstrating some gymnastic skills. Look for headstands, handsprings, and backflips in the beginning. Some of the more precocious will even try moving heavy appliances around the kitchen. Indulge them. This "superkid" phase will not last long.

BABY'S FIRST YEAR: what to expect during THE SEVENTH MONTH

By the seventh month your baby will abandon other
pursuits and get into non-stop drooling. You will
want to keep oxygen tanks and flippers handy lest
you get buried alive. You will also want to wear a
plastic raincoat at all times and keep the furniture
covered. You will also want to have galoshes
for visitors to wear. You will be miserable.
Baby will think it's a riot.

BABY'S FIRST YEAR: what to expect during THE EIGHTH MONTH

By now, baby should have decided that it has had enough sleep. "I have been sleeping for most of my life," baby will think to itself. "Enough is enough." It will not want to sleep any more. Consequently, you will not sleep any more. You will spend a lot of time crooning in front of the crib. You will spend a lot of time talking softly. You will spend a lot of time cursing under your breath. You will also spend a lot of time cursing out loud. Won't you be surprised when baby starts to talk!

BABY'S FIRST YEAR:
what to expect during
THE NINTH MONTH

This is a milestone month. Growing and bursting
with independence, baby will want to take on
increased responsibilities around the house. It may
even want to get a paper route. Don't be fooled by
this outward display of confidence, Baby will still
need your help doing such mundane things as filling
out its stock portfolio and choosing municipal
bonds.

BABY'S FIRST YEAR:
what to expect during
THE TENTH MONTH

The tenth month is a time of deep introspection for baby. Long, moody silences and solitary hours spent reflecting on life and its promise mark this period in baby's development. And there is so much for a young mind, poised on the verge of toddlerhood, to grapple with: Should I suck my thumb or should I get a security blanket? Should I toilet train early or should I wait and succumb to peer pressure? Should I be more like my Mom or more like my Dad? Which one is my Mom and which one is my Dad?

BABY'S FIRST YEAR: what to expect during THE ELEVENTH MONTH

We have walking. We have breaking. We have little fingerprints all over the furniture. We have things pulled out of drawers and a trail of destruction that makes the Johnstown flood look like an April shower. We have shoes. Real shoes.

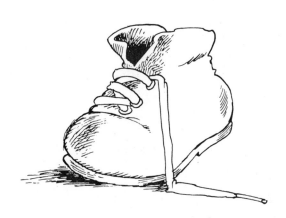

BABY'S FIRST YEAR: what to expect during THE TWELFTH MONTH

During the twelfth month an urbane and dapper little person will start to emerge as baby stands poised on the threshold of toddlership. Concern with appearance and personal grooming will become more evident, although the kid will continue to eat like a pig. Time to start applying to Ivy League schools. Your baby is growing up.

These other humorous titles are available at fine bookstores or by
sending $3.95 each plus $1.00 per book to cover postage and
handling to the address below.

Please send me:

QUAN.		TITLE
	5352-6	Skinny People Are Dull and Crunchy Like Carrots
	5370-4	A Coloring Book for Pregnant Mothers to Be
	5367-4	Games You Can't Lose
	5358-5	The Trite Report
	5357-7	Happy Birthday Book
	5356-9	Adult Crossword Puzzles
	5359-3	Bridget's Workout Book
	5360-7	Picking Up Girls
	5368-2	Games for the John
	5340-2	Living in Sin
	5341-0	I Love You Even Tho' . . .
	5342-9	You Know You're Over 50 When . . .
	5363-1	You Know You're Over 40 When . .
	5361-5	Wimps
	5354-2	Sex Manual for People Over 30
	5353-4	Small Busted Women Have Big Hearts
	5369-0	Games You Can Play with Your Pussy Cat (and Lots of Other Stuff Cat Owners Should Know)
	5366-6	Calories Don't Count If You Eat Standing Up
	5365-8	Do Diapers Give You Leprosy? What Every Parent Should Know About Bringing Up Babies
	5355-0	I'd Rather Be 40 Than Pregnant
	5362-3	Afterplay: How to Get Rid of Your Partner After Sex

Send me _____ books at $3.95 each $_____

Add $1.00 per book for shipping/handling   _____

Name_____

Address_____

_____

City/State/Zip_____

PUBLISHING COMPANY, INC,
125 Walnut St., Watertown, MA 02172
(617) 923-1111